ideals® COUNTRY

More Than 50 Years of Celebrating Life's Most Treasured Moments

Vol. 57, No. 3

Steep thyself in a bowl of summertime. —Vergil

IDEALS—Vol. 57, No. 3 May MM IDEALS (ISSN 0019-137X)
is published six times a year: January, March, May, July, September, and November by
IDEALS PUBLICATIONS INCORPORATED,
535 Metroplex Drive, Suite 250, Nashville, TN 37211.
Periodical postage paid at Nashville, Tennessee, and additional mailing offices.
Copyright © MM by IDEALS PUBLICATIONS INCORPORATED.
POSTMASTER: Send address changes to Ideals, PO Box 305300,
Nashville, TN 37230. All rights reserved.

Title IDEALS registered U.S. Patent Office.
SINGLE ISSUE—U.S. $5.95 USD; Higher in Canada
ONE-YEAR SUBSCRIPTION—U.S. $19.95 USD; Canada $36.00 CDN (incl. GST and shipping); Foreign $25.95 USD
TWO-YEAR SUBSCRIPTION—U.S. $35.95 USD; Canada $66.50 CDN (incl. GST and shipping); Foreign $47.95 USD

Subscribers may call customer service at 1-800-558-4343 to make address changes.
Unsolicited manuscripts will not be returned without a self-addressed, stamped envelope.

ISBN 0-8249-1161-X   GST 131903775

Visit *Ideals*'s website at www.idealspublications.com

Cover Photo
A Gardener's Bouquet
Nancy Matthews,
Photographer

Inside Front Cover
BRITTANY LANDSCAPE
Artist, Henry Moret
Superstock

Inside Back Cover
YOUNG FISHERMEN IN A ROWBOAT
Artist, Adam Emory Albright
Christie's Images

Country Noon
Grace V. Watkins

A summer noon should have a field of clover,
Red clover growing tall and sunlight sweet,
And velvet bumblebees cascading over
And buzzing down with pollen-dusty feet.
A honeybee's too small to probe a fat
Red clover bloom and take its ruddy measure;
Only a bumblebee can manage that
And calmly gather up the hidden treasure.
When summer comes, my heart will always go
Halfway across a continent and see
A hill where metronomes of time are slow
And hear a nectar-minded bumblebee
Lazily playing on his brown bassoon
Across the quiet of a country noon.

Fields of Clover
Vera Laurel Hoffman

Through the wide fields that are greening with clover
We have found peace beneath summertime's sun,
Watching the flight of the red-winged blackbird,
Noting the bees with their comforting hum.
High overhead clouds of cotton are drifting
As larksongs are carried for miles around.
We watch the butterflies bright as the flowers,
Gracefully floating and settling down.

Soft summer breezes are rippling the clover,
Weaving a soft song to gladden the heart,
Filling the day with a most-joyous splendor,
Making us glad that we're offered a part
Of all the wonder of sheer summer magic
With fields of clover to brighten the way.
We are well blessed in the glories of nature
As our hearts sing through the long summer day.

*Crimson clover floods California's Klamath Range.
Photo by Carr Clifton.*

Summer Interlude
Nora Bozeman

The blue sapphire skies bedazzle my eyes
And invite cotton clouds to go sailing.
The butterflies glide on magical wings
To welcome the day that's unveiling.

Red roses are kissed by the overnight mist
That has filled petaled cups full of dew.
A mockingbird sings his spontaneous song
To a summer day, golden and new.

The emerald grass with daisies amassed
Stands serene in the afternoon sun.
Leaves sigh in the breeze, caressing the trees
As if they will not be outdone.

I watch this display from my hushed hideaway
Till dusk bows to silver moonbeams;
Then I pack up my treasures and store them inside
My trunk full of summertime dreams.

Sweet Summer
Virginia Blanck Moore

Summer brings out cherries
For a pie that's sheer delight.
Summer brings out lightning bugs
To dot the velvet night.
Summer brings the perfume out
Of sweet pea and of rose.
Summer brings the freckles out
Upon a small boy's nose.
Summer brings wrens' melodies
And heat-dispelling breeze.
Summer—sweet, sweet summer—
Knows a thousand ways to please.

A nature preserve on the central Oregon coast blooms with checker-mallow and manroot. Photo by Bruce Jackson/Gnass Photo Images.

Overleaf: Pine trees thrive amid the rocky terrain of Providence Canyon State Park in Georgia. Photo by Gene Ahrens.

THE DAISY

James Montgomery

There is a flower, a little flower
With silver crest and golden eye,
That welcomes every changing hour
And weathers every sky.

The prouder beauties of the field
In gay but quick succession shine.
Race after race their honors yield;
They flourish and decline.

But this small flower, to nature dear,
While moons and stars their courses run,
Enwreathes the circle of the year,
Companion of the sun.

It smiles upon the lap of May,
To sultry August spreads its charm,
Lights pale October on his way,
And twines December's arm.

The purple heath and golden broom
On moory mountains catch the gale;
O'er lawns the lily sheds perfume,
The violet in the vale.

But this bold floweret climbs the hill,
Hides in the forest, haunts the glen,
Plays on the margin of the rill,
Peeps round the fox's den.

The lambkin crops its crimson gem;
The wild bee murmurs on its breast;
The blue-fly bends its pensile stem
Light o'er the skylark's nest.

'Tis flora's page, in every place,
In every season, fresh and fair;
It opens with perennial grace
And blossoms everywhere.

On waste and woodland, rock and plain,
Its humble buds unheeded rise.
The rose has but a summer reign;
The daisy never dies.

Shasta daisies intermingle with black-eyed Susans along a rural fence. Photo by William Johnson/Johnson's Photography.

Where innocent bright-eyed daisies are,
With blades of grass between,
Each daisy stands up like a star
Out of a sky of green.
— Christina Rossetti

From My Garden Journal

Deana Deck

OXEYE DAISY

In the Victorian language of flowers, the daisy is the symbol of innocence. It is not surprising, therefore, that we fill our childhoods with images of this simple flower. "Fresh as a daisy," our mothers croon as they whisk us from the bathtub and bundle our infant selves in soft, cushiony towels. "Daisy, Daisy, give me your answer, do," we sing around the summer campfire. "He loves me, he loves me not," young girls chant as they pluck a daisy's petals. June brides walk down the aisles wearing veils festooned with garlands of daisies or carrying bouquets of them tied in white ribbons.

Why then, when daisies are so common to everyday experience, is it difficult to find a genuine daisy to add to the garden? Daisies are not a rare or exotic species, but so many plants are called "daisy" that finding the one true form—the one you always picture when you hear all the quotes, poems, and songs—becomes a challenge. I became mired in this quandary when I was a novice gardener planning what I hoped would be a classic cottage garden, all wild with color, shape, and texture but firmly under control. Lush but simple— that was the goal.

I wanted to add daisies to the garden because they are a simple country flower, and it seemed to me they would be quite at home in a simple country garden. My few years of gardening had taught me that when it comes to color, an occasional glimpse of pure white among pinks, reds, and oranges provides contrast and rests the eye. Also, in the heat of midsummer, white flowers offer a fresh appearance.

Daisies are the most common of American flowers, and I thought they would be easy to locate. When I began my search, however, I was surprised to discover that many garden catalogs did not list them, and that garden books pictured a species with which I was unfamiliar.

One day, as I was thumbing through a new book on wildflowers, I discovered that I had been searching for the daisy by the wrong name. There, in full bloom on the book's pages, was the daisy I had been seeking, the real daisy. As it turns out, its common name is oxeye daisy, and it is a member of the vast chrysanthemum family—*C. Leucanthemum*, to be exact. To my surprise, I also learned it is not an American native.

C. Leucanthemum is native to most of

Europe, Northern Turkey, and China. Early settlers brought the daisy to America where it has naturalized throughout the continent. Hardy to Zone 5, the oxeye daisy grows in hay fields, along country roads, and across the grasslands of the West. In temperate climates it flowers from April to late June, but if it is cut back after flowering, then fed and watered generously, it will bloom again in the fall. It's an adaptable plant, with varieties found in a wide range of altitudes. It grows from a spreading rootstock and can be propagated by division, but it also grows from seed.

Usually, when a flower's botanical name is known, finding a particular species of flower is easy—not so with the oxeye. Most garden catalogs feature only some of the many hybrid perennial daisies. These flowers resemble the oxeye daisy, but like many hybrids, they do not share the tough wildflower stamina of the oxeye. For instance, the most popular of these is the Shasta daisy (C. x superbum), which does not fare well in hot climates. The oxeye daisy, common wildflower that it is, is even considered a weed by the United States Department of Agriculture. One pamphlet written by this agency, entitled *Lawn Weed Control*, provides directions for eradicating the oxeye daisy.

The oxeye daisy can be propagated by either dividing an existing plant or by collecting seeds from the dried blossoms as I finally did. Once the daisies began to go to seed, I snipped off the old blooms, and I left them to dry. When they were dried, I saved the seeds and planted them in the early spring.

I'd choose to be a daisy, if I might be a flower; Closing my petals softly at twilight's quiet hour.—Author Unknown

As you can imagine, any plant that will grow out in the middle of a meadow or along a dusty road isn't too particular about soil. Still, if you introduce your daisy plant to rich, well-drained garden soil, it will reward you with prolific blooms and hardy foliage for years to come.

Oxeye daisies are relatively disease and insect resistant. Some daisies, however, may be affected by powdery mildew in summer's hot humid weather. Mildew is the bane of all daisy types, but it can be controlled with fungicidal sprays. As for insects, few bother the oxeye, although you are apt to find the petals riddled by caterpillars from time to time. A spritz of neem oil in solution will stop this invasion.

The nice thing about oxeye daisies is that once they are established, they return year after year. Whether blown by wind or spread by small creatures, a new colony has sprung up quite on its own among the tangle of crown vetch, poppies, larkspur, and evening primrose that sinks roots into the soil at the edge of my lawn. This makeshift array of blossoms sways in the summer breeze, ready to greet the next young girl who passes by wondering if "he loves me or he loves me not." I feel a comfort in knowing that my real daisies are sure to know the proper answer.

Deana Deck tends to her flowers, plants, and vegetables at her home in Nashville, Tennessee, where her popular garden column is a regular feature in The Tennessean.

Summer in the South

Paul Laurence Dunbar

The oriole sings in the greening grove
   As if he were half-way waiting;
The rosebuds peep from their hoods of green,
   Timid and hesitating.
The rain comes down in a torrent sweep
   And the nights smell warm and piney;
The garden thrives, but the tender shoots
   Are yellow-green and tiny.
Then a flash of sun on a waiting hill,
   Streams laugh that erst were quiet;
The sky smiles down with a dazzling blue
   And the woods run mad with riot.

*The sun had bathed in golden dyes
This Southern land of sunny skies:
And crimson clouds, like birds of wing,
Did o'er the earth their radiance fling.*

—*Mary Weston Fordham*

The waters of Fall Creek Falls create a grand scene amid the surrounding Tennessee woodland. Photo by Gene Ahrens.

Barefoot Trails

Frank Fuis, Jr.

I long for trails through the wildwood shade
Where plays the cottontail unafraid
And leaps the squirrel from tree to tree,
Content at heart and blithe and free.

I long for fields and the open sky
Where crops are sweet and a brook runs by,
Where nature smiles in a thousand ways
On childhood fair in barefoot days.

I long to rest near a placid pool
Where moss is downy and damp and cool
And watch through whispering leaves on high
White bits of fleece go drifting by.

Oh, I must yield to this urgent call
To steal away to the rubble wall,
The vine-grown haunts, and the fence of rails
And roam once more those barefoot trails!

Summer Walk

Jessie Lofgren Kraft

One radiant afternoon
You took me down a green lane
For a jewel-like hour in June,
And the memory of that walk lingers—
The strong warmth of your hand
Closed over my child fingers,
The fragrance of catalpa blossoms,
    full blown and sweet,
The pungence of Bouncing-Betsy
    running in a riot
Of pink beneath our feet.
We stopped to rest on a mossy hillside
Where butterflies hovered.
Tenderly you untied
My sunbonnet, and the wind played
With my curls while you taught me
To whistle through a grass blade.

*Wildflowers tumble over the edge of a footpath
through Mynell Gardens in Jackson, Mississippi.
Photo by Dick Dietrich.*

COLLECTOR'S CORNER

Elizabeth Bonner Kea

For as long as I can remember, I have associated trout fishing with my grandfather. I was only five years old when Grandfather gave me my first fishing pole. We spent endless hours in his backyard as he taught me how to cast. When Grandfather finally deemed my talents worthy of the river, he took me to his favorite fishing waters—the Toccoa River in the Blue Ridge Mountains of Georgia.

Knee-deep in clear, cold water, I watched Grandfather's fishing technique. I marveled at his concentration and his patience as he waded through the river looking for the best place to cast. Grandfather possessed an uncanny ability to locate rainbow and speckled trout, both in the rapid currents of the river and in its shady recesses. Even more amazing, he knew what the fish would bite. Most often, Grandfather used crickets and corn as bait; but occasionally, if the fish were "finicky," as he called them, he would open his tackle box and carefully select a treat they could not resist. The chosen lure usually made me squirm a bit as I looked into its lifelike, glassy eyes and turned its rubbery form over in my hands. But the artificial bait almost always worked; we rarely went home empty-handed.

When I was an older and more experienced fisherwoman, Grandfather gave me my own magical lures to add to my tackle box. Each had various colors and particular characteristics which enabled me to catch many a "finicky fish." But it was not until the summer I turned thirteen that my grandfather gave me some truly magical lures—a collection of three Paw Paw Casting Minnows purchased from a Moonlight/Paw Paw Bait Company catalog in 1940.

"The catalog claimed," Grandfather told me, "that no game fish could resist this bait, so I bought three of them!" As I turned those unique lures over in my hands and observed the meticulously painted carved wooden heads and the red-feathered tails, I began to understand a little of the history of angling. These lures represented some of the early prototypes in man's quest to tempt a fish to his hook. Grandfather had already taught me the sport of fishing; now he was sharing its art.

With that small gift of three, I embarked on a hobby of collecting antique fishing lures. I read every book on lures, I looked for interesting designs, and I learned to appreciate craftsmanship. Although most antique fishing lures were made over only a forty year span, those produced varied in color, material, size, detail, and shape. I have chosen, for the most part, to collect lures manufactured by the Moonlight/Paw Paw Bait Company. This focus keeps me from being overwhelmed by the many lures from which to choose. Though I do not pursue collecting as an investment as others might do, I always enjoy the thrill of finding a lure whose box and papers read "Paw Paw, Michigan" across the bottom.

Most of my lures are worth very little by collectors' standards; I do not pursue the most sought-after pieces, but focus on lures that have detailed designs. Displayed in a wooden box, I have baits made of wood, metal, and even deer hair, with two- and three-pronged hooks. Some have small propellers attached, whereas others have unique shapes that enable them to twirl through the water. All of my lures have qualities that intrigue me, but invariably, in perusing my collection, my eyes return to the three Paw Paw minnows that inspired this hobby. I look at them and wonder how many trout Grandfather caught using them and if he ever encountered a fish who could resist them. Now, I can rarely get away for a fishing trip, but just a few moments spent with my collection bring a flood of memories: of the Toccoa River, of speckled trout, and of Grandfather, who gave me a love of the sport—and the art—of fishing.

TACKLE TALK

If you would like to collect antique fishing lures, the following information will be helpful.

HISTORY

• Prior to the mid-1800s, most lure makers developed simple lures that repeatedly twisted through the water like propellers. But angling history soon gave way to the "lure designers" who crafted animated, lifelike bait intended to tempt the human eye as much as the fish's appetite.

• The first patented American fishing lure, the Buel Arrowhead Spoon, was developed by Juleo T. Buel in 1852.

• The region stretching from Ohio to Michigan is often referred to as the "lure belt." Out of this Great Lakes area emerged the "big ten" lure manufacturers that would produce the most well-known handcrafted lures between 1900 and 1940.

• Following World War II, the manufacturing of fishing lures became more efficient with the introduction of machinery capable of producing thousands of lures a day. Artisans who spent hours brushing seven to fourteen coats of paint on each lure were replaced with modern equipment able to perform the same job in minutes.

COLLECTING

• Research is an important prerequisite to collecting. In the past few years, several experienced lure collectors have authored antique fishing lure guidebooks which provide estimated values of lures and other helpful information.

• The desirability of an antique lure is determined by vintage, rarity, and condition.

• When attempting to identify a lure's manufacturer or age, collectors typically observe the hook rigs, propellers, and eye detail of the lure.

• Novice collectors can often be overwhelmed and discouraged by the vast market of collectible lures. For this reason, most long-time collectors suggest directing a collection according to company, vintage, design, material, or color.

• According to the National Fishing Lure Collector's Club grading system, the condition of an

Antique fishing tackle holds memories of more than just the one that got away. Photo courtesy of Rick Edmisten, co-author of Fishing Lure Collectibles.

antique lure may be rated on a scale of zero to ten, with zero being poor and ten being excellent. Generally, if a lure is unused with its original box, it is considered in excellent condition, but a lure that has parts missing or has been repainted is considered in poor condition.

INTERESTING FINDS

• Some collectors have the unique opportunity to discover "experimental lures," those lures that failed to become a marketable product, but nevertheless survived in a company's archive or an employee's tackle box.

• Handmade lures, though difficult to value monetarily, provide a collector with an unusual piece of American folk art. Their uninhibited design and crude features can provide a refreshing contrast to the repetitive appearance of commercial lures.

Life at the Lake

James Whitcomb Riley

The green below and the blue above!
The waves caressing the shores they love:
Sails in haven and sails afar
And faint as the waterlilies are
In inlets haunted of willow wands,
Listless lovers, and trailing hands
With spray to gem them and tan to glove.
The green below and the blue above.

The blue above and the green below!
Would that the world were always so!
Always summer and warmth and light,
With mirth and melody day and night!
Birds in the boughs of the beckoning trees,
Chirr of locusts and whiff of breeze,
World-old roses that bud and blow.
The blue above and the green below.

The green below and the blue above!
Heigh! young hearts and the hopes thereof!
Kate in the hammock and Tom sprawled on
The sward—like a lover's picture, drawn
By the lucky dog himself, with Kate
To moon o'er his shoulder and meditate
On a fat old purse or a lank young love.
The green below and the blue above.

The blue above and the green below!
Shadow and sunshine to and fro.
Season for dreams, whate'er befall
Hero, heroine, hearts and all!
Wave or wildwood, the blithe bird sings,
And the leaf-hid locust whets his wings
Just as a thousand years ago.
The blue above and the green below.

In Maine's Baxter State Park, the stillness of Daisey Pond reflects Mount Katahdin. Photo by Dianne Dietrich Leis.

BITS & PIECES

The merry fish are playing
Adown yon crystal stream.
—Thomas J. Ouseley

From beneath his dark haunt beneath the tangled roots
Of pendant trees, the monarch of the brook
Behoves you then to ply your finest art.
—James Thomson

I shall stay him no longer than to
wish that if he be an honest angler,
the east wind may never blow when
he goes a-fishing.
—Izaak Walton

Angling is somewhat like poetry;
Men are to be born so.
—Izaak Walton

He's angling for trout in a
tumbling brook, and his lessons
are all forgot.

—George R. Hayler

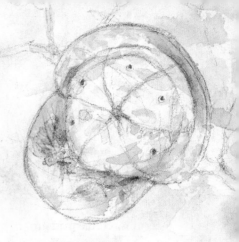

Oh, the gallant fisher's life!
It is the best of any;
'Tis full of pleasure, void of strife,
And 'tis beloved by many.

—Izaak Walton

Of recreation there is none
So free as fishing is, alone;
All other pastimes do no less
Than mind and body, both possess:
My hand alone my work can do;
So I can fish and study too.

—William Basse

I have laid aside business, and gone a-fishing.

—Izaak Walton

I want the dawn's first gleaming dim
To waken something deep in him.
I want my boy to learn to take
His troubles to that shining lake
And lose them there; and so I wish,
O son of mine, that you may fish.

—Author Unknown

An outing together for father and son
Affords loads of pleasure 'fore even begun.
For in planning the trip is found half of the sport;
And when it is finished, seems always too short.

—Louis T. Wood

MY LADDIE

Wilbur D. Nesbit

You have to grow up, my laddie, and wander
    away from me,
Up and down through the field and town and
    over the calling sea.
The fun-tangled curls that you wear today
Will change into hair that is shot with gray.
So laugh, you, my laddie, and sing and play
Or ever you go from me.

You haven't a care, my laddie; the world is a
    wondrous place
With play and song the whole day long, and
    nothing is mean and base.
So keep it as long as your heart beats light
And view every dawn as a marvel-sight.
The day will be here when your toil will write
Its story upon your face.

You've got to grow up, my laddie, and wander
    away from me
Up and down through the field and town, and
    out on the tossing sea.
But now you are little, and life is good,
So wring out its rapture, as well you should;
So laugh, you, my laddie—I wish I could
The day that you go from me!

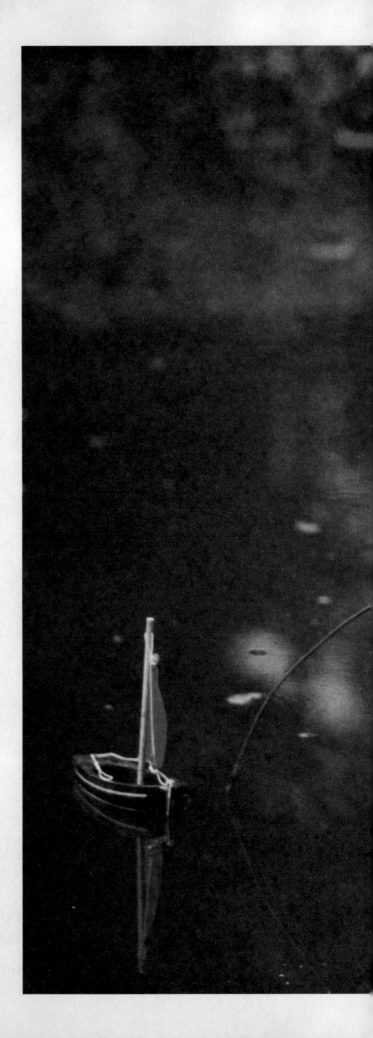

*A young boy dreams of sailing a bigger sea in this image
from Telegraph Colour Library/FPG International.*

If

Rudyard Kipling

If you can keep your head when all about you
Are losing theirs and blaming it on you;
If you can trust yourself when all men doubt you,
But make allowance for their doubting too;
If you can wait and not be tired by waiting,
Or being lied about, don't deal in lies,
Or being hated, don't give way to hating,
And yet don't look too good, nor talk too wise:

If you can dream—and not make dreams your master;
If you can think—and not make thoughts your aim;
If you can meet with Triumph and Disaster
And treat those two impostors just the same;
If you can bear to hear the truth you've spoken
Twisted by knaves to make a trap for fools,
Or watch the things you gave your life to, broken,
And stoop and build 'em up with worn-out tools.

If you can make one heap of all your winnings
And risk it on one turn of pitch-and-toss,
And lose, and start again at your beginnings
And never breathe a word about your loss;
If you can force your heart and nerve and sinew
To serve your turn long after they are gone,
And so hold on when there is nothing in you
Except the will which says to them, "Hold on!"

If you can talk with crowds and keep your virtue,
Or walk with kings—nor lose the common touch;
If neither foes nor loving friends can hurt you,
If all men count with you, but none too much;
If you can fill the unforgiving minute
With sixty seconds' worth of distance run,
Yours is the earth and everything that's in it,
And—which is more—you'll be a man, my son!

A loyal twosome work their land in THE FARMER AND HIS SON AT HARVESTING
by artist Thomas Pollock Anshutz. Image from Christie's Images.

HANDMADE HEIRLOOM

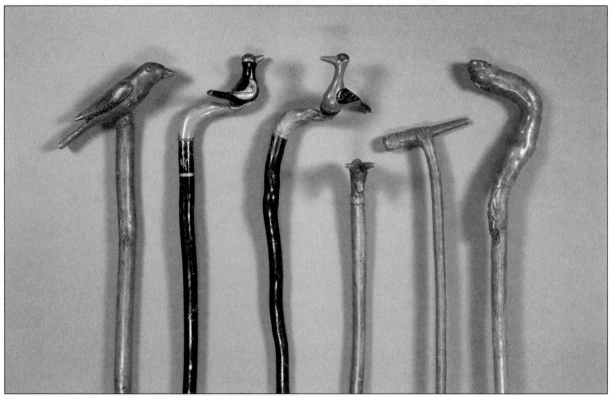

An assortment of walking sticks carved from 1885 to 1910 reflects the patience of their maker, who carved in Berks County, Pennsylvania.

HANDCARVED WALKING STICK

Nevin Shaw

I learned to carve from my father, who was a real woodsman; born more than eight decades ago, he lived his entire life in the north country of New Hampshire. He carved mostly wood, but he also collected discarded deer antlers for special projects. I remember walking the early winter woods with him, before the snow fell, in search of these abandoned treasures—no longer needed by the deer who had shed them, but prized by collectors and carvers. When winter came, I would spend endless afterschool hours in my father's workshop, watching as he transformed these antlers, and the carefully selected branches and saplings he'd collected during the summer and fall, into art. He carved delicate jewelry, animal figurines, simple musical instruments, canes, boxes, and more. I loved the way he handled his tools

with such ease and confidence, the way the tiny, controlled strokes of metal on wood or antler would slowly reveal shapes hidden within. That is what it seemed like to me, that the shapes that he carved were not the products of his imagination, but forms trapped within the piece in his hands, forms that awaited his magical touch to emerge. I didn't ever consciously think of Father as an artist; but that is what he was, a man not only skilled with the physical tools of carving but gifted with a true artistic vision.

Father worked quietly. I learned not by listening to his instructions, but by watching. He was peaceful at his work, almost eerily so. Only every now and then would he offer a word or two of spoken instruction, and there were days when I felt almost as if my presence were a distraction to him. But that was my father, a man of very few words. So I watched and absorbed and learned.

When I was ten years old, my father announced that I was ready for my first solo project. I had handled the tools before. I had even carved some simple work with my jackknife on discarded ends of wood and antler; but now, Father said, I was ready to make something entirely on my own. He suggested a wooden walking stick, and I readily agreed, eager to begin and to please. On an early fall day we took to the woods, searching, he told me, for just the right sapling. He wasn't as concerned with the type of tree as with the shape and sturdiness of the young trunk. He finally settled upon a maple sapling no more than two inches in diameter that rose about three feet from the ground before curving to accommodate a second branch. "This will do," he said and then instructed me to cut it down at ground level. Back at the workshop, Father began to explain, step by step, how to clean and prepare my sapling for carving. I had seldom heard so many words come from his mouth, and I gathered them in, eager to follow his guidelines by the letter.

I worked slowly and carefully with my jackknife, just the way I had seen my father work. He showed me how the natural curve at the top of the sapling would make a perfect hand grip for my walking stick, and I whittled and chipped until the piece felt smooth and fit comfortably in my hand.

When the project was finished, I was impressed with my work. Father simply said, "Fine job." But I know he was pleased too. I had listened well over the years; and although my work was certainly that of a beginner, it was beautiful to both of us. From that day on, I always carried that stick on walks in the woods with my father. I felt like I had crossed some sort of bridge, and I guess I had. Father launched me on more and more difficult carving projects, and my love of the art grew. One by one he passed his old tools on to me, building my tool collection as he watched my skill grow. I learned to use the gouges and chisels along with my jackknife and learned to clean, sharpen, and care for these sturdy, well-used tools the way Father did. Today, I have a workshop of my own, actually much bigger than my father's, in the basement of my home. I follow his example in caring for and storing my tools, and I know that when he visits my home, he takes great pride in seeing my carving room. I don't think I have ever reached his level of artistry, but I am as devoted as he was to the art of carving.

All of these memories have been much on my mind lately. I have decided to teach my own son to carve. He has, of course, been watching me for years, ever since he was five years old and proved himself old enough to be quiet and safe around my carving tools and workshop. And I have tried to emulate my father's teaching methods. I have tried to work quietly and skillfully, to teach by doing not by speaking. I don't know if I have succeeded at that. Often as not my son and I have spent our time in the workshop talking: about school, about sports, about friends. Sometimes I have told him stories about his grandfather, about my own childhood. It has been nice, but not like the silence I remember. But every now and then there will be a pause in the conversation, and I will see him watching my hands work. On those occasions I imagine he is feeling what I used to feel watching my father, that he is trying to absorb my skills and knowledge.

My son is ten now, about the same age I was when I carved my first walking stick. So we have been walking the woods, searching for a sapling. My dream is that he will carve his own walking stick and we will bring it together to his grandfather, who is no longer able to carve because of failing vision. I imagine how proud my son will feel and how pleased his grandfather will be to see that his craft has been passed down. And of course I will be proud of him, and I will be hoping that Father is proud of me. I will never grow out of that. Most of all, I imagine that for a moment or two we three generations of men will be united by our love of carving.

This is a grand dream, I know, a lot to expect from a simple sapling carved into a walking stick. But as I walk the woods with my son, a boy who is more familiar with computers than with maples and birches, I feel the strangest sense that I have been here before. I see him watching me, wanting to learn. I hear my father's words come from my own mouth. I see time and years and generations melt away in this shared moment between a man and a boy as we carry on this age-old art of carving.

THE SUSTAINING

Grace V. Watkins

My father was a quiet man and shy,
Uneloquent in any spoken phrase,
As unassuming as the winds that sigh
Across the prairie where I spent the days
Of childhood, and as lowly as the grain
Upon that wide and sun-illumined plain.

But when my father read the holy Word,
His voice was like a golden waterfall,
So filled with love and worship to the Lord
That we who listened were sustained for all
The years to be, however gray the storms,
Secure within the everlasting arms!

Brilliantly colored paintbrush sweeps over a field in Independence, Texas. Photo by William Johnson/Johnson's Photography.

I REMEMBER FATHER

Minnie Klemme

I remember flowers
In my father's hand
As he came at even
From the prairie land.

I remember sunshine
On my father's face,
Smiles and happy laughter,
And his fond embrace.

I remember goodness
In my father's heart;

Would I had his wisdom,
Could the same impart.

I remember music
In my father's voice;
I would be just like him
Could I have my choice.

I remember father
With a wistful sigh
For a prairie flower
And the days gone by.

A Man Apart

Minnie Klemme

There was a field, well-fenced with wooden rail,
Where in the spring the lark and oft the quail
Would mark my steps as down the track I came
To bring my father water in a pail.
There I would sit beside the furrow's end
And listen to the train come round the bend.
The while I watched the horses drawing near,
Still pulling strong the rich black earth to tend.

Then we would watch the freight trains rolling by,
Return the wave of trainmen with a sigh,
And dream of cargoes bound from coast to coast,
And follow far the smoke with wistful eye.
My father had adventure in his heart—
The right-of-way was like an open chart—
He spoke of cities far along the line;
I knew by then he was a man apart.

Like horse and plow, he too was of the land;
The silver rails were not at his command.
He ate his bread with sweat upon his brow;
His feet were chained, but heart and eye oft scanned
The sweep of fields beyond the river's edge.
He knew horizons I had never seen,
Strange ships at sea beyond the sage and sedge.

And sometimes with his poet's eye he'd find
Things close at hand and often call to mind
The ways of ant and bee among the grass,
A ladybug and others of its kind.
His hands were gentle with a broken wing;
For him there was no bird too mean to sing.
The field mouse and the rabbit were his friends—
His soul was freshened by an endless spring.

The wild rose was to him the world's perfume;
At eve the glowworm lit the friendly gloom.
And when he sifted soil through thoughtful hands,
He knew no chains, nor were the fields his doom.
Now at the furrow's end, his work well done,
The native earth reclaims her poet son.
His soul is free to venture to its home;
His body blends with fallow soil and loam.

And I, who am his child, now find my heart
Is chained where his was free—no busy mart
Can take the place of fields with furrows plowed;
Again by silver rails must I depart.

*A streamtrain stops for passengers in Lancaster County, Pennsylvania.
Photo by M. Burgess/H. Armstrong Roberts.*

Devotions FROM THE Heart

Pamela Kennedy

"If I rise on the wings of the dawn, if I settle on the far side of the sea, even there your hand will guide me, your right hand will hold me fast." Psalm 139:9, 10

LIVING IN A FOREIGN COUNTRY

Emily came to work every day with an expression of sadness on her face. Her steps were slow and her shoulders slumped as if bearing a heavy weight. When I asked her what was bothering her, she said, "I hate it here. I don't have any friends. I wish we had never moved. I miss everything about my old home."

When Mary's youngest child left for college, Mary complained, "I feel so useless and empty. Life has just lost its joy."

Bill's life changed dramatically after a car accident. His back ached constantly, and there was a numbness in his right arm the doctor said might be permanent. "Where was God when this happened?" he asked. "I'm an artist, and I can hardly hold a paintbrush now. What am I supposed to do?"

Emily, Mary, and Bill were all in places they didn't want to be—geographically, emotionally, and physically. Each one of them felt far from God, alone, and unhappy. There are times when we too may feel displaced, alone, or frustrated. It's a little like being in a foreign country—a place where the landscape is unfamiliar and the language difficult to understand. Changes in locations, families, friends, or health can cause us to wonder if God knows or cares where we are and what we are going through. At times we may even feel that we have moved away from God, or He from us.

In Psalm 139, David reminds us that there is no place we can go to escape God's loving care. David

Dear heavenly Father, thank You for Your promise to be with me in every situation and circumstance. When I am feeling afraid or lonely, please help me to know the comfort of Your hand, guiding and holding me fast.

knew what he was talking about. As a young person, David was called to leave the familiar pastures of Bethlehem for the royal palace where he played his harp for a depressed and moody king. Later, that same king, consumed with jealousy and rage, forced David to bid farewell to his dearest friend, Jonathan. For years, David lived as a fugitive in constant danger, dwelling in caves and tents, unable to return home. He knew what it was to be among strangers, to long for family, to despair and wonder if God cared about him. But David also knew how to pray. And in his prayers he reached out to grip with faith the hand of his Lord. It was at a time like that when David composed the comforting words of Psalm 139. And his words speak to our hearts as well.

Whether we experience heavenly joy or the depths of despair, God is with us in every circumstance. Even more wonderful is the fact that His care is very personal. Unlike a guidebook or a roadside sign pointing the way, our heavenly Father is intimately involved in our journeys and holds us tightly each step of the way. When we feel we are in a place where no one knows or understands our concerns, we need only reach out in prayer to grasp the ever-open hand of our Lord. There is no country where He is not present. There is no place on heaven or earth where His love cannot reach.

The sun sets beyond the Heceta Lighthouse in Oregon's Devils Elbow State Park. Photo by Dennis Frates.

WITH GRANDFATHER

Margaret Boulay

Here I sit upon the porch
And watch the sun come up.
My grandfather also sits,
In hand his coffee cup.

"The morning is a beauty,"
Is what he says to me.
Together we both gaze upon
The dew, the birds, the trees.

The air is fresh and crisp today;
The sun is warm above.
I share this time with Grandfather;
This time is what I love.

ON THE PORCH WITH GRANDPA

Constance Hollingshead

Every summer evening, after a supper of cold fried chicken and sun-ripened tomatoes, Grandma would plunge my hot, sticky body into a galvanized tub of cool water. She'd scrub my hide until it turned red and gently dry me in a giant thirsty towel. To complete the ceremony, she would dip an enormous pink powder-puff into her own concoction of rice powder and jasmine and dust me until I sneezed; she said this precaution was necessary so I wouldn't get heat rash.

Once Grandma and I had finished our ritual and said goodnight, I would slip on my white palisse nightgown with the tiny pink rosebuds, give her a hug, and pad off to the front porch.

My grandpa and I had this game we played every night. I would slip silently out the wooden screen door, being very careful not to let it bang, then tiptoe across the wide, gray-painted boards and ease my freshly scrubbed and powdered body slowly onto the porch swing and cuddle up next to the rough blue overalls that encased the most wonderful man I'd ever known, my grandpa.

We would sit quietly and gently swing for awhile with his arm securely around me, and then he would say, "My, the night-blooming jasmine sure smells sweet tonight." He would give me a squeeze and look down at me and in a surprised voice say, "How long have you been here? I didn't hear you come out." And I would giggle.

Together we'd watch the darkness creep up the little valley and softly cover the surrounding countryside. First Ed Parks's sheep barn would disappear. Then the small white church with its tall steeple pointing out the North Star would be hidden within the folds of night; unless it was Wednesday, when its stained-glass windows would spill light on the darkened grass while the voices of the choir drifted on the summer breeze.

Sometimes Grandpa and I would talk about different things, other times he'd tell me stories about my mother when she was a little girl. But mostly we'd watch the sheet lightning dance across the distant horizon and the tiny fireflies dip and sway, performing their light show to a concert of crickets, frogs, and katydids—each celebrating the jasmine-scented evening.

Above left: A grandfather and granddaughter share a well-loved story. Photo by Rob Gage/FPG International.
Above: A porch swing invites dreams to grow. Photo by Jessie Walker.

Feet

Dorothy Aldis

There are things feet know
That hands never will:
The exciting pounding feel
Of running down a hill;

The soft, cool prickliness
When feet are bare
Walking in the summer grass
To most anywhere;

Or dabbling in water all
Slip-sliddering through toes—
(Nicer than through fingers, though why
No one really knows.)

"Toes, tell my fingers," I
Said to them one day,
"Why it's such fun just to
Wiggle and play."

But toes just looked at me
Solemn and still.
Oh, there are things feet know
That hands never will.

Two young farmhands cool their feet after a run through the pasture in COOL DELIGHT *by artist Donald Zolan. Copyright © Zolan Fine Arts Ltd., Hershey, Pennsylvania.*

Note on Kitchen Table

Mary Martin Palma

I will be back soon to bake some bread,
But now I'm picking wild berries instead,
Out in the meadows, under the sun.
I know I'm leaving my work undone,
But the wind was soft on summer grass;
The trees stood up tall for me to pass;
And the blue sky smiled and bent down low.
So what could I do but laugh and go?

The First Wild Strawberries

Marion Doyle

If there is any smell to equal this,
I've never found it—
No mortal Merlin
Ever bound it
In crystal vials.
Creation dials
June,
And to the tune
Of flicker and of cricket,
Down the road
I go,
Past haw and wild plum thicket.
Where lately white stars glowed
Upon the vines,
The red fruit shines
Warm in the sun.
I will, I say,
Taste one, just one.
Alas!
Down in the grass
Like Nebuchadnezzar
On my knees
Devour
Compound of shower,
Earth, and sun—
Dozens and scores!
What have I done?
Eaten them greedily,
Every one.
Not even conscience could prevail,
And home I go—with empty pail.

Artist Eloise Harriet Stannard (1828–1915) recreates the lusciousness of summer's bounty in STRAWBERRIES IN A WICKER BASKET ON A LEDGE. *Image from Christie's Images.*

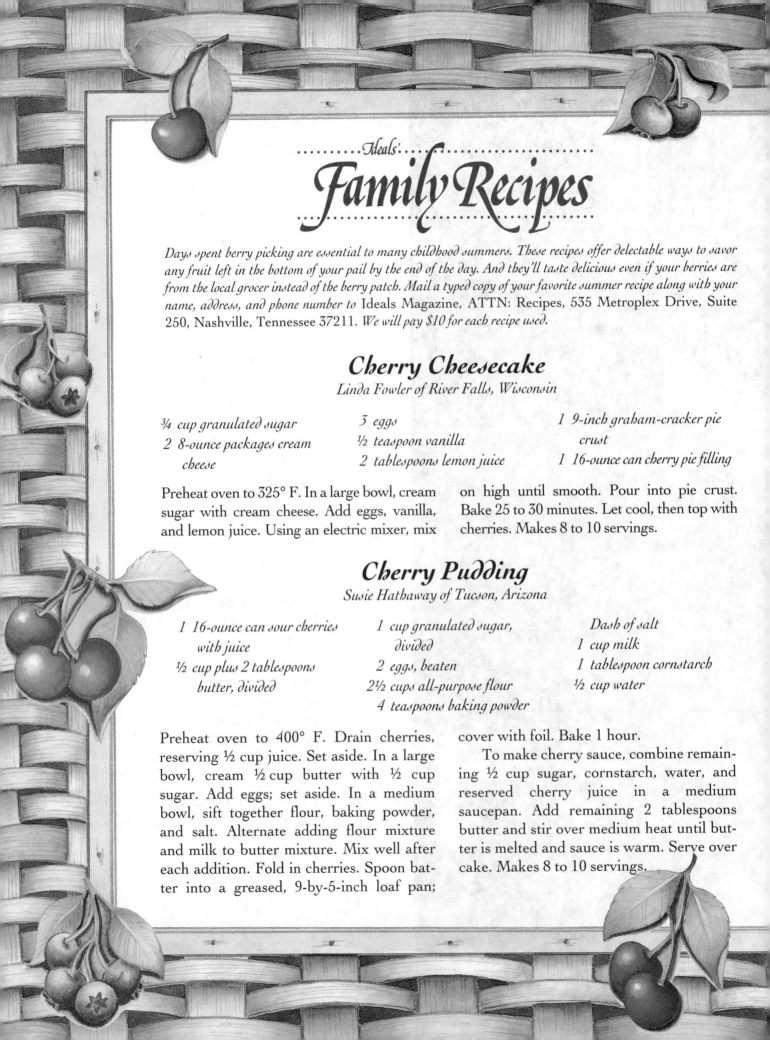

Ideals'
Family Recipes

Days spent berry picking are essential to many childhood summers. These recipes offer delectable ways to savor any fruit left in the bottom of your pail by the end of the day. And they'll taste delicious even if your berries are from the local grocer instead of the berry patch. Mail a typed copy of your favorite summer recipe along with your name, address, and phone number to Ideals Magazine, ATTN: Recipes, 535 Metroplex Drive, Suite 250, Nashville, Tennessee 37211. We will pay $10 for each recipe used.

Cherry Cheesecake
Linda Fowler of River Falls, Wisconsin

¾ cup granulated sugar

2 8-ounce packages cream
   cheese

3 eggs

½ teaspoon vanilla

2 tablespoons lemon juice

1 9-inch graham-cracker pie
   crust

1 16-ounce can cherry pie filling

Preheat oven to 325° F. In a large bowl, cream sugar with cream cheese. Add eggs, vanilla, and lemon juice. Using an electric mixer, mix on high until smooth. Pour into pie crust. Bake 25 to 30 minutes. Let cool, then top with cherries. Makes 8 to 10 servings.

Cherry Pudding
Susie Hathaway of Tucson, Arizona

1 16-ounce can sour cherries
   with juice

½ cup plus 2 tablespoons
   butter, divided

1 cup granulated sugar,
   divided

2 eggs, beaten

2½ cups all-purpose flour

4 teaspoons baking powder

Dash of salt

1 cup milk

1 tablespoon cornstarch

½ cup water

Preheat oven to 400° F. Drain cherries, reserving ½ cup juice. Set aside. In a large bowl, cream ½ cup butter with ½ cup sugar. Add eggs; set aside. In a medium bowl, sift together flour, baking powder, and salt. Alternate adding flour mixture and milk to butter mixture. Mix well after each addition. Fold in cherries. Spoon batter into a greased, 9-by-5-inch loaf pan; cover with foil. Bake 1 hour.

To make cherry sauce, combine remaining ½ cup sugar, cornstarch, water, and reserved cherry juice in a medium saucepan. Add remaining 2 tablespoons butter and stir over medium heat until butter is melted and sauce is warm. Serve over cake. Makes 8 to 10 servings.

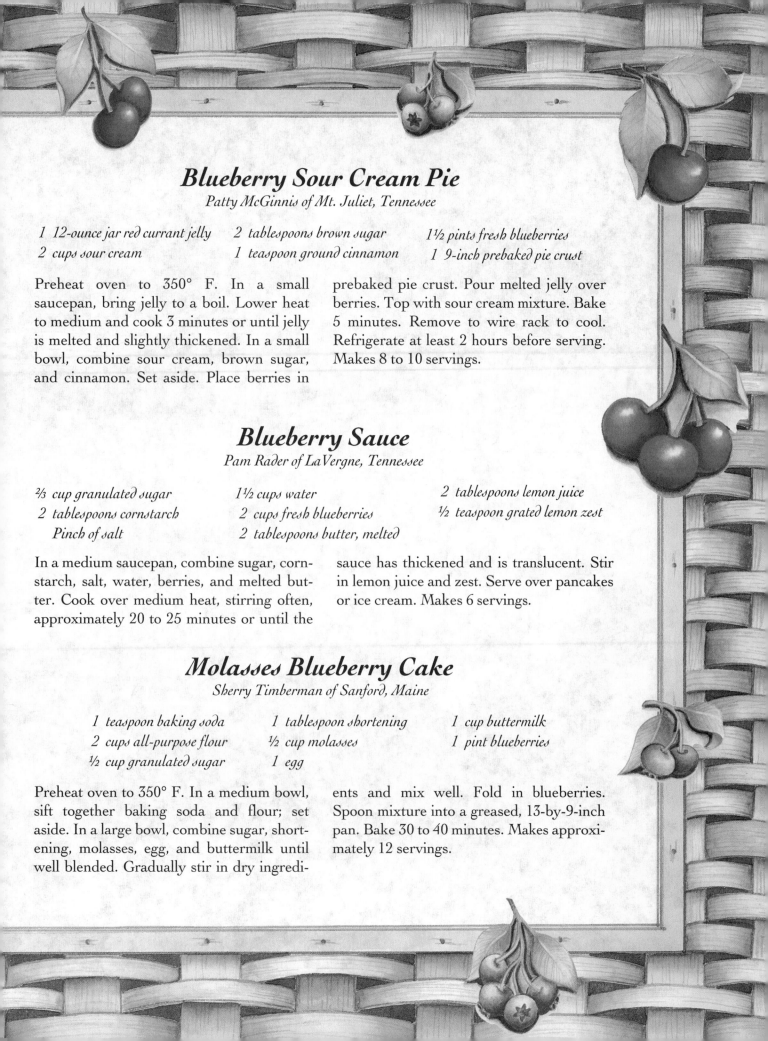

Blueberry Sour Cream Pie
Patty McGinnis of Mt. Juliet, Tennessee

1 12-ounce jar red currant jelly

2 cups sour cream

2 tablespoons brown sugar

1 teaspoon ground cinnamon

1½ pints fresh blueberries

1 9-inch prebaked pie crust

Preheat oven to 350° F. In a small saucepan, bring jelly to a boil. Lower heat to medium and cook 3 minutes or until jelly is melted and slightly thickened. In a small bowl, combine sour cream, brown sugar, and cinnamon. Set aside. Place berries in prebaked pie crust. Pour melted jelly over berries. Top with sour cream mixture. Bake 5 minutes. Remove to wire rack to cool. Refrigerate at least 2 hours before serving. Makes 8 to 10 servings.

Blueberry Sauce
Pam Rader of LaVergne, Tennessee

⅔ cup granulated sugar

2 tablespoons cornstarch

Pinch of salt

1½ cups water

2 cups fresh blueberries

2 tablespoons butter, melted

2 tablespoons lemon juice

½ teaspoon grated lemon zest

In a medium saucepan, combine sugar, cornstarch, salt, water, berries, and melted butter. Cook over medium heat, stirring often, approximately 20 to 25 minutes or until the sauce has thickened and is translucent. Stir in lemon juice and zest. Serve over pancakes or ice cream. Makes 6 servings.

Molasses Blueberry Cake
Sherry Timberman of Sanford, Maine

1 teaspoon baking soda

2 cups all-purpose flour

½ cup granulated sugar

1 tablespoon shortening

½ cup molasses

1 egg

1 cup buttermilk

1 pint blueberries

Preheat oven to 350° F. In a medium bowl, sift together baking soda and flour; set aside. In a large bowl, combine sugar, shortening, molasses, egg, and buttermilk until well blended. Gradually stir in dry ingredients and mix well. Fold in blueberries. Spoon mixture into a greased, 13-by-9-inch pan. Bake 30 to 40 minutes. Makes approximately 12 servings.

A Barn Is Never Quiet

Lon Myruski

A barn is never quiet 'gainst
The crimson streaks of dawn
When chanticleer, upon his perch,
Croons acappella songs
With vibrant voice that soon bestirs
Farm creatures great and small,
Who moo and murmur, squeal and sigh
From stanchions, pens, and stalls.

A barn is never quiet when
Its weathervane squeaks round
Beguiling cooing pigeons with
Gay, hurdy-gurdy sounds.
And peckish nestlings chirp for food
From rafters near and yon—
Beseechings ringing blissfully
Like cabaret chansons.

A barn is never quiet 'neath
The sable midnight sky
When raindrops tap the tin-clad roof
Composing lullabies
While hooting owls lend harmony
And sing their night away—
A cycle of enchanting sounds
That air anew each day.

An old barn and pasture are brightened by a border of blossoms in Polk County, Oregon. Photo by Steve Terrill.

LIFE IN ITS ABUNDANCY

Florence Marie Taylor

"Easy Dan, old boy." The gray horse clops
Contentedly, hoof-deep in soft, brown soil.
The farmer thrills to feel the pull of reins
Within his hands—to look up from his toil
At the feather whiteness of the clouds that quilt
The blue. Sweet fragrance is an old delight
Relived, born from red-fruited apple boughs.
And there is joy in hearing sudden flight
Of quail flushed from rose brambles by the fence.
The clover meadow and the questing bee,
The rows of young corn gleaming in the field—
This is life in its abundancy.
And strength grows deep within the heart of a man
Whose toil unites the whole world in its span.

*No race can prosper until it learns
that there is as much dignity in
plowing a field as in writing a poem.*

–Booker T. Washington

FARMER JOHN

Gail Brook Burket

He swung the heavy pasture gate,
Unhurried as the sun.
All other work would have to wait
Until the chores were done.
He knew the ways of earth revealed
No cause to rush or shove.
The blossoms in his clover field
Grew sweet as April love.
For God and he believed it wrong
To try to hurry hay;
They worked together, calm and strong
From dawn to dusk each day.
Like golden hymns, the fields of grain
Praised God's beneficence
Of mellow loam, the sun, and rain,
And John's great diligence.

*Horses rest after a day of labor at a farm near Bessemer City,
North Carolina. Photo by Norman Poole.*

A SLICE OF LIFE

Edgar A. Guest

THE SUMMER CHILDREN

I like 'em in the winter when their cheeks are slightly pale;
I like 'em in the springtime when the March winds blow a gale.
But when summer suns have tanned 'em and they're racing to and fro,
I somehow think the children make the finest sort of show.

When they're brown as little berries and they're bare of foot and head,
And they're on the go each minute where the velvet lawns are spread,
Then their health is at its finest and they never stop to rest.
Oh, it's then I think the children look and are their very best.

We've got to know the winter, and we've got to know the spring;
But for children, could I do it, unto summer I would cling.
For I'm happiest when I see 'em as a wild and merry band
Of healthy, robust youngsters that the summer sun has tanned.

Edgar A. Guest began his illustrious career in 1895 at the age of fourteen when his work first appeared in the Detroit Free Press. *His column was syndicated in over three hundred newspapers, and he became known as "The Poet of the People."*

ELEPHANTS ON MAIN STREET

Marjorie Holmes

In our small town, theatrical events were scarce but steady. And there were advantages. With only one thing going on at a time, you never had to make choices. That was *it*. And when it was over, the spell lasted; you had time to linger over its memory even as you began looking forward to the next.

In winter the pickings were fairly slim. Vaudeville once a month after the movies; the emotion-charged speaking contests at the high school; and a big home-talent musical sponsored almost every year by the Chamber of Commerce. But summer, ah, in summer! You could count on a carnival in summer, usually around the Fourth of July. Every few years a circus came to town (I doubt if we could have stood the excitement more often)—Sells Floto, Yankee Robinson, Clyde Beatty, or lesser ones. Size didn't matter; a circus, any circus, was so awesome, so alien, so exotic it was scarcely to be believed. To think that wild animals would actually be roaring and pacing their cages in our midst, that acrobats and bareback riders would be performing in somebody's pasture! We never felt that a circus belonged to us like Chautauqua or Sweets Show, or even visiting carnivals or the Alta Fair in the fall; a circus was a kind of incredible visitation.

The circus usually arrived in the night, and Dad would get us up to go down and watch them unload (especially in the years when we couldn't scrape up the money for tickets). Lots of other people had the same idea—there was always a crowd of parents holding sleepy children or leading them by the hand. It was exciting but scary, the hooting whistles, the clanking and squealing as cars were

"Come quick, elephants on Main Street, elephants in the lake!" Everybody ran. It was like suddenly being catapulted into a chapter of The Jungle Book.

switched about, the waving of lanterns and flashlights, and torches whose tarry smell mingled with the rank citric odor of beasts. Thrillingly, on a siding, was a long line of dark cars where, oblivious to all this, the performers slept.

How could they, in all the commotion? Strange-looking men trudged purposefully about, opening boxcar doors, leading horses down the ramp—and zebras and Shetland ponies—like a line of animated toys. Others drove the great teams of workhorses that were to pull the wagons and the cages. Cages that now waited, ominous and frightening and mostly silent—but now and then a hyena screamed, a lion roared.

"Where are the elephants, Daddy?" a child would ask. "I want to see the elephants." Then everybody would cry out, "Here they come!" Impossibly huge, their gray shapes flowed past in the night, on toward the pasture where some of them would be put to work hauling tent poles. Excitedly we would follow, to watch them moving with amazing grace and precision under the lights. Hammers rang, making a melody of three notes as three roustabouts alternately struck the stakes that held the ropes. Then up it rose, the great white Big Top blossoming, while all about it like some magical garden the smaller tents sprang into being.

The parade was the next day at noon, and this too was almost too impressive. It staggered the senses—the horses straining at the painted wagons; the band in its gold braid and plumes, playing from its high, richly ornamented carriage; the beautiful, bored-looking girls lurching along on elephants in gilded trappings; the cages with their pacing tawny beasts—all that pomp and splendor moving down

To the delight of young and old, a parade of elephants is led down Main Street. Photo by Deutsche Presse/Archive Photos.

Main Street! Past the courthouse and the post office and the banks, past the barbershop and the two cafes and the pool hall and the stores. The steam calliope was last, and its wild plaintive notes were somehow appropriate, eerie, and unsettling.

Sometime during the day came another spectacle, entirely free. The elephants were herded down to the lake to be watered. Along the street they plodded, toward the football field and the ice houses, there to wade in, dipping and lifting their serpentine trunks, sometimes trumpeting joyfully as they gave themselves showers. We didn't live far and word traveled fast. "Quick, come quick, elephants on Main Street, elephants in the lake!" Everything was dropped, everybody ran, and keeping a respectful distance, stood open-mouthed. It was like suddenly being catapulted into a chapter of *The Jungle Book*.

The circus left a kind of glittering ache in the air; like anything unusual, it aroused our longings. Overnight, trapezes and tightropes appeared in yards, our bagswings jolted to newer, more death-defying leaps.

My children have never had to get up in the night to watch the circus unload because they couldn't afford admission to the performance. They have color TV and stereo sets; they can attend concerts, see plays traditional or in the round. But I doubt if they have ever experienced the absolute, unadulterated delight we knew in entertainment.

I am glad I was raised in a little town at a time when things didn't happen very often, but when they did they happened grand. I wish, just once, my children could see elephants on Main Street!

Old Farmer at the Five and Ten

Edna Jaques

A gray old farmer at the five and ten—
Picking up little gadgets as he goes,
A painted hook, a few assorted bolts—
Counts out a few small screwnails that he knows
Will come in handy out around the place,
A look of sheer delight upon his face.

He buys a button for the smokehouse door,
Tests out a saw with a well-calloused thumb,
Picks up a little whetstone in a box,
Hunts for a hinge with flanges smooth and plumb,
Chuckles with glee at some new-fangled whim
That seems to strike a funny spot in him.

He makes his way around the crowded aisles,
Tut-tutting in a mild bewildered way,
Fingering the little gadgets bright and new,
His simple heart pleased at the wide display
(Like a small boy loose in a country store
Wondering what he will spend his pennies for).

He digs around in an old shabby purse
To find the money for his little bill,
Smiles at the girl in an old gentle way
Who drops the money in the clicking till.
Then down the street he goes as pleased as punch,
Back where he left the car, to eat his lunch.

Many a farmer in Catawba County, North Carolina, has visited Murray & Minges Country Store, established in 1890. Photo by Norman Poole.

My Land

Fred Toothaker

Where the turf lies green and the streams run clear
And the birch trees gleam with their white veneer,
Where the air stays pure and the skies stay blue
While the sun shines bright and the clouds are few,
That's my land.

Where the soil bed's rich in a fertile earth
To produce the crops that are treasure worth,
Where the climate's such that it stimulates
And the rainbow shows when the storm abates,
That's my land.

Where the corn stands tall in an August sun
And the wind blows soft till the harvest's done,
Where the days are warm and the nights are cool
And the folks all practice the golden rule,
That's my land.

Where the sun sets red and the dawn comes bright,
And it makes you feel that the world's just right,
Where the roots go deep to a moisture bed
To resist a drought that may lie ahead,
That's my land.

Where the friends you make are the friends you'll keep,
And the seeds you sow are the seeds you'll reap,
Where the neighbors help when it's help you need,
While it matters not what your faith or creed,
That's my land.

The Tahquamenon River rushes over the falls in Luce County, Michigan.
Photo by Darryl Beers.

THE STARS AND STRIPES

Roy Z. Kemp

It is our flag, a noble inspiration,
The banner of a nation that is free.
It sings of pride, of honor, faith, and glory,
A heritage of valiant victory.

It never fails to stir the pulse and heart
When it comes proudly waving down the street;
God, may it never fall, become dust-laden
And trodden down by tyrants' cruel feet!

May all its meaning never once be hidden
Nor shattered by some heartless, cruel foe.
But may its radiance be always gleaming
Before the world, wherever men may go.

Long may it wave and wend its thrilling message
From mountaintop to shore of shining sea.
Our Stars and Stripes! Long may it wave above us,
Proud symbol of our country's liberty.

THE FLAG

Helen Welshimer

The wings of the ships that sail the sky
And the vessels that cruise the seas,
The tramp of feet where long armies come
And the wind in the singing trees,
The odor that comes from soil, new-turned,
The hum of machinery's wheel,
A soldier's blood and a woman's faith,
Courage and dreams and steel.

Out of their warp the day is made,
Out of their web there comes
The banner that floats when brave men march
To the tune of the martial drums.
May we have strength to keep it high.
God, let no dull threads mar
The flag of a thousand victories,
Keep it a guiding star.

*The Stars and Stripes wave over a barn in Warwick, New York.
Photo by Scott Barrow/International Stock.*

OUR HERITAGE

AMERICA

Samuel Francis Smith

My country, 'tis of thee,
Sweet land of liberty,
Of thee I sing;
Land where my fathers died,
Land of the Pilgrim's pride,
From ev'ry mountainside,
Let freedom ring.

My native country, thee,
Land of the noble free,
Thy name I love;
I love thy rocks and rills,
Thy woods and templed hills,
My heart with rapture thrills,
Like that above.

Let music swell the breeze,
And ring from all the trees
Sweet freedom's song;
Let mortal tongues awake;
Let all that breathe partake;
Let rocks their silence break,
The sound prolong.

Our father's God to Thee,
Author of liberty,
To Thee we sing;
Long may our land be bright;
With freedom's holy light,
Protect us by Thy might,
Great God, our King.

ABOUT THE TEXT

When Reverend Samuel Francis Smith of Amherst, Massachusetts, wrote the song that would become our national hymn, he had no grand ambitions for his work. Asked in 1831 by the renowned music educator and hymn-writer Lowell Mason for a patriotic school song, Smith turned to the familiar tune of the British national anthem and wrote his new lyrics in a single sitting. The song, entitled "America," debuted shortly thereafter at a children's Fourth of July celebration in Boston. Listeners immediately embraced Reverend Smith's quiet song, and it has since remained a patriotic standard to all who appreciate the blessings of this land and nation.

In North Carolina, an American flag flies high atop Chimney Rock, part of the Blue Ridge Mountains. Photo by Norman Poole.

This Is My Country

Harry Elmore Hurd

This is my country—mine to keep
Within my heart until I sleep
Too soundly to give heed to song
Beyond my window. I belong
Within these borders bounded by
New England walls and mountain-high
Horizons. You who do not know
The drifted loveliness of snow
Upon these glacial hills deride
These pinelands greening to the tide
That rose and broke, historically,
Against a rock in Plymouth. Key
Your laughter to the sterner note
Of men, unmusical, who smote
On granite with the ancient rod
Of Moses—watering the sod
With faith abundant for their needs.
I love this soil where even weeds
Grow beautifully as goldenrod
Or chicory, and faith in God
Is adamant as are the hills
From whose aloofness summer spills
The grace of rain upon the land
Where whispering rows of cornstalks stand
In fertile valleys. Here my heart
Abides. I am an integrant part
Of stubborn soil: my roots are here
Where man companions with the deer
And shares the vesper sparrow's song
At silver eventide. I belong
To Yankeeland where neighbors are
The strong-limbed offspring of a star.

*A coastline covered in granite and spruce overlooks
Frenchman's Bay in Maine's Acadia National Park.
Photo by William Johnson/Johnson's Photography.*

Lines on Revisiting the Country

William Cullen Bryant

I stand upon my native hills again,
Broad, round, and green, that in the summer sky,
With garniture of waving grass and grain,
Orchards and beechen forests basking lie,
While deep the sunless glens are scoop'd between,
Where brawl o'er shallow beds the streams unseen.

A lisping voice and glancing eyes are near,
And ever restless feet of one, who, now,
Gathers the blossoms of her fourth bright year;
There plays a gladness o'er her fair young brow,
As breaks the varied scene upon her sight,
Upheaved and spread in verdure and in light.

For I have taught her, with delighted eye,
To gaze upon the mountains, to behold
With deep affection the pure, ample sky
And clouds along its blue abysses roll'd,
To love the song of waters and to hear
The melody of winds with charmed ear.

Here, I have 'scaped the city's stifling heat,
Its horrid sounds and its polluted air;
And where the season's milder fervors beat,
And gales that sweep the forest borders bear
The song of birds and sound of running stream,
Am come a while to wander and to dream.

Ay, flame thy fiercest, sun! thou canst not wake,
In this pure air, the plague that walks unseen.
The maize leaf and the maple bough but take,
From thy strong heats, a deeper, glossier green.
The mountain wind, that faints not in thy ray,
Sweeps the blue streams of pestilence away.

The mountain wind! most spiritual thing of all
The wide earth knows—when, in the sultry time,
He stops him from his vast, cerulean hall,
He seems the breath of a celestial clime;
As if from heaven's wide-open gates did flow,
Health and refreshment on the world below.

*Left: Elk graze in a meadow below Mount Rundle in
Canada's Banff National Park. Photo by Dennis Frates.
Above: A boy surveys the countryside he will one day tend.
Photo by Telegraph Colour Library/FPG International.*

Candle Lilies

Mildred Moon Howell

Tiger lilies spread their flame
On tall candle stems,
Casting shadows on the grass,
Clutching at their hems.
And the flame burns high or low
With each soft breeze blowing,
Meshed of sunlight, caught and held
In the twilight glowing.
Tiger-lily candles hold
All of Midas's treasured gold.

Gracious as sunshine, sweet as dew shut in a lily's golden core.
—Margaret J. Preston

Tiger Lilies

Thomas Bailey Aldrich

I like not lady's-slippers,
Nor yet the sweet-pea blossom,
Nor yet the flaky roses,
    Red, or white as snow;
I like the chaliced lilies,
The heavy Eastern lilies,
The gorgeous tiger lilies
    That in our garden grow!

For they are tall and slender;
Their mouths are dashed with carmine,
And, when the wind sweeps by them,
    On their emerald stalks
They bend so proud and graceful.
They are Circassian women;
The favorites of the Sultan
    Adorn our garden walks.

And when the rain is falling,
I sit beside the window
And watch them glow and glisten.
    How they burn and glow!
Oh, for the burning lilies,
The tender Eastern lilies,
The gorgeous tiger lilies
    That in our garden grow!

Two elegant stalks of tiger lilies stand refreshed after a summer shower. Photo by William Johnson/Johnson's Photography.

Nancy Skarmeas

MCRAE

CELIA THAXTER

A celebrated Childe Hassam painting from the late nineteenth century shows poet Celia Thaxter dressed all in white, standing alone in her garden on New Hampshire's Appledore Island. In the distance are the blue waters of the Atlantic. It is this image of Thaxter that her devoted readers have always cherished: she is the "island poet"—a strong and solitary woman who found inspiration for her writing on an isolated island. But life for Celia Thaxter was never as serene as it appears on Hassam's canvas. Although the "island poet" loved nothing more than island life and the sea, she in fact found her first poetic inspiration as a land-locked, lonely, over-burdened young mother living miles away from the roar of the Atlantic, and she spent much of her life in unfulfilled longing to return to the islands of her childhood. In the full story of Celia Thaxter's life, Hassam's painting illustrates only one chapter.

Celia Laighton Thaxter was born in 1835 in Portsmouth, New Hampshire; but the childhood of her memory was to be spent on the Isles of Shoals, ten miles out in the Atlantic, where her father, Thomas Laighton, took his family in 1839 when he assumed the post of lighthouse keeper on White Island. Thomas Laighton fell firmly under the spell of island life. He later worked as an innkeeper on nearby Appledore Island and never returned to live on the mainland. Celia grew up with the island and the sea as her playground and classroom. The sound of the surf, the touch of the wind, the smell of salt air, the cold harsh winters and short but glorious summers—all of these provided the backdrop for a unique and idyllic childhood.

Not until she was sixteen years old, married, and expecting her first child did Celia Thaxter begin to understand the hold that island life had upon her. Her husband, Levi Thaxter, did not love the sea as she did, and he took his young bride to live in Newtonville, Massachusetts. Living fewer than twenty miles from the Atlantic coast, Celia nonetheless felt land-locked and detached in Newtonville. She spent summers with her family on Appledore; but as a married woman, convention declared that her home was wherever her husband decided to make it. Thus Thaxter remained most of the year in Newtonville. Celia loved her three sons and was devoted to their care, but her husband proved an unreliable provider and a frequent wanderer. Overwhelmed by the demands of motherhood, by the separation from her family, by the growing distance between herself and her husband, Celia began to long even more strongly for the islands of her childhood.

As the years passed, Celia Thaxter discovered that within her longing also lay her inspiration, and she secretly began to write poetry. In 1860, Levi Thaxter came upon one of his wife's poems and sent it to a friend at *The Atlantic Monthly* magazine. Levi never gave in to his wife's desire to return to the island, but he saw in her poetry the opportunity for family income. The poem, called "Land-locked," was accepted and published. The verses spoke eloquently of Thaxter's undeniable longing to return to the sea and how that longing often made it hard for her to appreciate the beauty and richness around her. "Land-locked" was an instant success and secured for Thaxter a reputation as one of America's rising literary stars. And for Celia Thaxter, it was the beginning of a professional writing career that would help lift her out of despair.

American readers embraced Celia Thaxter, and her work was also admired by the leading literary figures of the day. The young poet soon numbered James Russell Lowell, John Greenleaf Whittier, and Sarah Orne Jewett among her friends. She published poems in magazines of the day, including *Harper's*, *Century*, *Scribner's*, and pieces for children in *St. Nicholas*. She also published two book-length collections of poetry in 1872 and 1873. Although she more often than not penned her verses from her inland home in Massachusetts, she wrote about the sea, her gardens, and the birds and animals of Appledore. She wrote as if she looked out her window each day upon this pristine island world. But in truth, she did not.

Levi Thaxter supported his wife's writing career but not her desire to live permanently on the islands. Celia spent summers on Appledore at her family's inn and she played host there to her many new literary friends, but the Thaxters never had a permanent island home of their own. Increasingly as the years passed, Celia and Levi led separate lives—she on the island during the summer, he in Florida during many winters. The closest Thaxter ever came to having her own home in the Isles of Shoals was the house she and Levi purchased in 1880 in Kittery Point, Maine. From there she could look out over the Atlantic toward her beloved islands.

Celia Thaxter had both profound sorrow and great joy in her life. She grieved over the distance in her relationship with her husband, and she worried until her last days over the fate of her eldest son Karl, who was born mentally ill. But she saw two of her sons mature into happy and successful young men; she made close and dear friends in the literary society of her day; she saw her poetry embraced by the readers of a nation; and she found peace always on Appledore, where she devoted endless hours to a garden that would become nationally known and celebrated in her book, *An Island Garden*, and where she soaked up the sounds, smells, and images that enlivened her verse.

By the end of the 1880s, Celia Thaxter was perhaps the best-known and best-loved of America's women poets. She was firmly established in the American imagination as the "island poet," and her cherished Appledore and garden were as famous as she was. She held regular "salons" for her literary friends, who gathered to read their work and to be enriched by each other's company. Thaxter had achieved success and notoriety beyond any of her dreams, and she made for herself a life that was happy and fulfilling.

Celia Thaxter's poetry, sometimes still included in anthologies, especially those for children, is no longer widely known. But there are those who still consider her one of America's best poets, and her memory remains vivid in the minds of these devoted admirers. There is a museum on Appledore, not far from where Thaxter was buried after her death in 1894, that draws thousands of tourists each summer. There are societies across the nation organized in her name, and several groups—one as far away as Colorado—have worked to recreate her famous Appledore Island garden. Celia Thaxter's modern-day admirers celebrate her not only as a poet, but as a gardener, a bird-expert, an accomplished cook, and a china-painter. They remember her as a woman of independent spirit, a woman who decided not to give in to the frustrations that gripped her as a very young wife and mother, but instead to turn her deep feelings into beautiful verse.

It is likely that when these admirers, so familiar with Thaxter's struggles and accomplishments, look upon Childe Hassam's beautiful painting, they see an artist's work brought to life by the spirit of his subject. They see their beloved "island poet"—a woman who in truth lived much of her life land-locked and longing for the sea—at home at last in her ocean-side garden with the comforting roar of the surf in her ears. For those familiar with the life and work of Celia Thaxter, Childe Hassam's painting comes alive with the spirit of a remarkable woman.

Land-locked

Celia Thaxter

Black lie the hills; swiftly doth daylight flee;
And, catching gleams of sunset's dying smile,
Through the dusk land for many a changing mile
The river runneth softly to the sea.

O happy river, could I follow thee!
O yearning heart, that never can be still!
O wistful eyes, that watch the steadfast hill,
Longing for level line of solemn sea!

Have patience; here are flowers and songs of birds,
Beauty and fragrance, wealth of sound and sight,
All summer's glory thine from morn till night,
And life too full of joy for uttered words.

Neither am I ungrateful; but I dream
Deliciously how twilight falls tonight
Over the glimmering water, how the light
Dies blissfully away, until I seem

To feel the wind, sea-scented, on my cheek,
To catch the sound of dusty flapping sail
And dip of oars, and voices on the gale
Afar off, calling low—my name they speak!

O Earth! thy summer song of joy may soar
Ringing to heaven in triumph. I but crave
The sad, caressing murmur of the wave
That breaks in tender music on the shore.

The Pemaquid Point Lighthouse welcomes seafarers to Maine's shores.
Photo by Daniel Dempster.

Renowned Impressionist artist Childe Hassam captured this scene of Celia Thaxter in her garden in 1892. The painting, entitled In the Garden, *is one of Hassam's many illustrations for Thaxter's book* An Island Garden. *Image from National Museum of Art/Art Resource, New York.*

TRAVELER'S Diary

APPLEDORE ISLAND AND THE ISLES OF SHOALS

Off the coast of Portsmouth, New Hampshire, stands Appledore Island, one of the Isles of Shoals and the home of poet Celia Thaxter and her remarkable garden. Acclaimed in articles such as the one below from an 1874 edition of Harper's New Monthly Magazine, *Thaxter's garden is described in detail in her 1894 book,* An Island Garden. *Today, a replica of Thaxter's garden is tended by an outpost of Cornell University, and boats still carry visitors to Appledore to share its beauty.*

My first visit to the Isles of Shoals was made in mid-August. The grass had everywhere the emerald brightness of the first June days, before the sun has parched it or the dust has dimmed its glory. But the emerald of the grass was outrivaled by the sapphire of the sea. The fact that it was Sunday made the natural stillness of the day more evident. I had driven down from Portsmouth, past many a field already sumptuous with goldenrod, to a point of land at the extreme mouth of the river and directly facing the Shoals.

I strolled down to the last extremity of the land and looked out over the flashing sea to the group of islands two or three leagues away. But for the great houses upon Star and Appledore, they would have made a very little break on the horizon. I had been reading Celia Thaxter's little book about them. How strange it seemed, so looking at them, that they should have inspired so much enthusiasm, so much poetry—that they should have been the scene of so much comedy and tragedy and eventful life!

The next day I took the handsome little boat that plies between Portsmouth and Appledore. We glided on until we reached the open sea and struck out for the slowly lifting bulk of Appledore. The house at Appledore stretches its long veranda across the head of a little cove. A little to the left of the "lordly pleasure-house" is the cottage where Mrs. Celia Thaxter, the princess of this Thule, holds her court. In front of Mrs. Thaxter's cottage is the flower garden which she has celebrated in her book, and this August day it was a splendid rage of color, the flame of the nasturtiums leaping everywhere among the poppies and sweet peas, the corn-flowers and the

marigolds. The sun that shines upon these barren ledges and the winds that visit them seem not only to "Touch the human countenance/ With a color of romance," and to make blanched cheeks ruddy once again, but to bestow on every flower that blooms upon the Isles a color that its kindred on the main can seldom boast.

The air of Appledore is full of spicy scents of shrubs and tiny plants—scents more delicious than homecoming ships from Spain ever brought with them to these Isles. There were places where I hardly dared to tread for fear of crushing out a colony of the delicate houstonia, and the more delicate trientalis was growing all about, and the pretty stone-crop, and I knew the pimpernel was not far off.

And still the glory of these islands is not in anything that clothes the rocks, but in the rocks themselves. If they could be stripped bare of every scrap of green they nourish with precarious food, they would be just as grand as they are now, though far less beautiful; for their soft grays and browns wed very happily with the scanty grass and foliage and bring forth exquisite effects of color.

After having stayed here for a few days the towns and cities of the continent become a dream, a myth, to you. One's experience here begets a feeling that our ordinary world is too large. In the course of the forenoon a fresh breeze from the south sprang up, and I bade good-by to my gracious hosts and went on board the *Molly*, who very soon spread her white wings and made straight for Portsmouth Harbor. And I said in my heart, I have enjoyed so much that I must tell my joy to others, if haply they may enter into it, and perchance follow my example.

Shell-Bound

Doris Acree

I love all the sea-touched things:
The flowing tide that moonlight brings;
The wheeling seagull as it sweeps for prey;
The grey salt mist of early day;

White gleaming cliffs, blue-tinged;
Secret inlets, sandy fringed;
And seaweed lying moist on shores
For weathervanes to hang indoors;

And salty spray that drops
In curling strands from green wavetops.
Within this pearled and polished shell,
I hold the sea I love so well.

Another Sound

Darrell T. Hare

She put the shell against her ear.
Then rising from her knee,
She closed her eyes and, pressing hard,
She listened for the sea.

I knew she heard the water roar;
She glowed with childish pride.
To hold the ocean in her hand
Was more than she could hide.

She ran across the sand to me;
I listened for a while
Then tucked the shell within her hand
And nodded with a smile.

I thought that she could learn from me,
But who am I to tell?
She brought the ocean home today;
I only brought a shell.

A young girl explores the wonders of the sea in
SEASIDE DISCOVERY *by artist Eve DeGrie.*

Readers' Reflections

The Sea and Me
Wilma Heideman
Cincinnati, Ohio

Today I sat beside the sea
And heard the waves sing songs to me.
A gentle breeze caressed my skin;
The healing of my soul begins.
And this I know (for mortal me)
I'm close to heaven
By the sea.

Walk to the Beach
Joanne B. Smith
Lake Harmony, Pennsylvania

We walk to the beach with
Folding chairs, blankets, towels,
Food baskets, bare feet,
Bouncy hair, hats, sunglasses,
Buckets, shovels, and cut-off jeans,
Bathing suits, cover-ups,
Baby carriages, beach umbrellas.
We have
Brown hands, smiling faces,
A regimen across the busy street, walking
down the ramps setting up camp.
While there
We swim, sun, raft, talk, lounge, eat,
Sleep, build castles, buy ices, jump waves.
Where is this wondrous, memorable day?
Locked within.

Day at the Beach
Lois Weiss
Beloit, Wisconsin

Waves break against the sandy shore.
Children laugh and run barefoot,
Clad in rainbows of color
That cling to their wet skin.
Castles of sand appear
Under their skillful hands,
Only to disappear again
Under the trampling of their feet.

Mystic Sea

Nancy Browning
Jackson, Tennessee

Flowing ebbtide
Running free,
Shimmering waves
Of the rolling sea.

Hypnotic lure
On shifting sand,
Breezy balm
In splendor grand.

Tempestuous winds,
Blustery roar
In awesome wonder
And exotic lore.

Mysterious sea
Of fathoms deep
Enraptures the soul
In shrouded mystique.

Secrets engulfed
In waters green,
Never revealed
Nor seldom seen.

Ever gushing,
Rarely serene,
Rolling, lapping.
Where have you been?

Sifting Sand

Pam Iseley
Greensboro, North Carolina

I love to hear the sound
Of crashing waves upon the shore,
Even though I've heard it all
One thousand times before;
And if I live one thousand years,
I'll love to hear it evermore.

There's something about the rhythm,
As the breakers wax and wane,
That soothes the weary, stress-filled soul
Like the patter of the rain
And leaves a comforting exhilaration
That will linger and remain.

I love to walk a sunny beach
With my husband, hand in hand,
As rivulets of salty water
Gently bathe the land
And sift the sand beneath our feet
On the shoreline where we stand.

I love to get away from man-made
Dwellings for a while
To contemplate the sounds of nature
Or life on a distant isle
And let the surging of the tide
Restore my soul and reconcile.

Editor's Note: Readers are invited to submit unpublished, original poetry for possible publication in future issues of Ideals. *Please send typed copies only; manuscripts will not be returned. Writers receive $10 for each published submission. Send material to Readers' Reflections, Ideals Publications, Inc., 535 Metroplex Drive, Suite 250, Nashville, Tennessee 37211.*

THROUGH MY WINDOW

Pamela Kennedy

Art by Eve DeGrie

AN ISLAND SUMMER

After two decades of living on urban Navy bases, our second son announced that he wouldn't be coming home from college to work at the car lot where he had spent previous summers detailing automobiles. He was tired of city life. He wanted to find a job in the country, where he could enjoy nature and live at a slower pace. Perhaps, he suggested, he would find a job in a national park or forest where he could commune with nature and escape the rat race. His father, ever the practical economist, argued that Smokey the Bear would probably not pay as well as the rats. And I suggested

that for someone of his age and energy level, communion with nature can be highly overrated! But our son remained undaunted.

For several months, he sent out resumes and inquiries to parks, camps, and resorts in remote areas with disappointing results. Then he called us in April to announce he had found the perfect job. He and his roommate had been hired to work at a bed and breakfast called Deer Harbor Inn on Orcas Island located in the Stratis of Juan de Fuca, between Washington State and Canada. Orcas was accessible only by private plane and ferry boat and well known for its abundant wildlife and pristine beauty. The boys would be doing general maintenance around the inn during the day and working in the small dining room in the evenings, washing dishes and bussing tables. In their free time they would be able to explore the island and surrounding waters. It sounded like the perfect setting for our son's foray into country life.

By mid-summer, we were able to take a vacation and decided to include a couple of days at Deer Harbor. Intrigued by our son's reports of its beauty and peacefulness, we wondered if he had really found what he was looking for on this isolated island. After all, this was the kid who wasn't happy without the newest piece of computer equipment, the latest movies, and tickets to attend concerts of newly emerging bands. Was there really a country mouse lurking deep inside him? In July, we determined to find out.

We drove onto the ferry at Anacortes, Washington, and climbed to the observation deck for the two-hour ride to Orcas. As the white and green vessel glided through the water, we were captivated by the beauty of evergreen-covered islands slipping by on either side. Seagulls swooped overhead, calling to one another in scolding tones as they rode the gusting summer wind. The crisp salt air filled our lungs, and we laughed in delight to see a school of sleek black and white killer whales frolic in sun-splashed waves. Sailboats and kayaks skipped through the water leaving trails of white foam, and hundreds of buoys bobbed offshore, marking the hopes of those who planned to feast on crab or shrimp.

After disembarking on Orcas Island, we followed our son's directions, driving down a winding two-lane road dappled by sun and shadows that played through the evergreen branches. He was waiting as we arrived at the inn, anxious for us to get settled so he could take us on a tour of his favorite haunts. In the two days we spent with him, we canoed on pristine lakes and along salt-water shorelines, climbed an observation tower high on the island's east side for a breathtaking view, and heard tales of our son's encounters with the local wildlife. He told us how he had watched a pair of bald eagles fighting talon to talon in a summer sky one morning and

how a playful sea otter stole the salmon-head bait out of his crab pot, then boldly splashed him as he sat reading in the afternoon sun. He recalled an evening when he and a friend sat as still as statues in an old apple orchard while half a dozen deer wandered in to eat the fallen fruit, and the time they had to frantically paddle their canoe to escape the currents rushing through Pole Pass. On hot afternoons, they leapt from the branches of a huge Douglas fir into the pure, fresh water of a spring-fed lake then dried off on sun-warmed boulders. The island residents and summer guests seemed friendlier than their city counterparts, he mused, and island life had a totally different texture. We realized he had found what he had longed for—a place that nurtured not only his body, but his soul as well.

And as we spent time together, we understood how much we had unwittingly become creatures of the city, forgetting about the lessons one learns in the country. There in the overwhelming stillness of the night, the stars are closer and brighter. The breezes, scented with warm pine needles and ripening berries, are sweeter, and the bonds between earth and man are stronger. There, if only for a season, our son had discovered life moving at a different pace. There he could pause to marvel at the exquisite pulsing beauty of an orange jellyfish or the sharp contrast of black and white on a breaching whale's back. In the forest, the symphony of bugs and birds and breezes played, uninterrupted by man or machinery. There was time to hike, to reflect, to wonder.

There is a strength in knowing a place like Orcas Island, if only for one brief summer; a strength that comes from learning there are more than manmade miracles in the world. Long before the time of cyber-space and microchips, there was the time of the country, a time of land and sea and sky. I am so glad our son had the determination to search for it—and when he had found it, that he invited us to rediscover it as well.

Pamela Kennedy is a freelance writer of short stories, articles, essays, and children's books. Wife of a retired naval officer and mother of three children, she has made her home on both U.S. coasts and currently resides in Honolulu, Hawaii.

To a Seabird

Bret Harte

Sauntering hither on listless wings,
    Careless vagabond of the sea,
Little thou heedest the surf that sings,
The bar that thunders, the shale that rings—
    Give me to keep thy company.

Little thou hast, old friend, that's new;
    Storms and wrecks are old things to thee.
Sick am I of these changes too;
Little to care for, little to rue—
    I on the shore and thou on the sea.

All of thy wanderings, far and near,
    Bring thee at last to shore and me.
All of my journeyings end them here:
This our tether must be our cheer.
    I on the shore and thou on the sea.

Lazily rocking on ocean's breast,
    Something in common, old friend, have we:
Thou on the shingle seekest thy nest,
I to the waters look for rest—
    I on the shore and thou on the sea.

A group of seabirds enjoys a spot in the sun in this painting entitled Sea Gulls *by artist Arkadij Aleksandrovic Rylov (1870–1939). Image from Museum of Art, Kiev, Russia/Superstock.*

God's Laundry

Edna Moore Schultz

God strung a row of snowy birds
Across a southern sky.
The scene, quite undescribed by words,
Enraptured from on high
Like oceans tide, formation changed
As if by soft command.
The motion, as they rearranged,
Seemed uniformly planned.

Perhaps God hung the birds aloft
Where wind could blow them dry.
He may have fluffed their feathers soft
Like pillows in the sky.
I wonder if He used a bleach
To give them extra sheen.
I mused about it on the beach
As I beheld the scene.

God placed each feathered one in line;
I know not how nor when.
I only know the view was mine
To savor there and then.
They flew with strength and purpose sure
Til distance blurred the sight.
They brought, before they were obscure,
Brief moments of delight.

Who Owns This Field
Anne Campbell

I do not know who owns this field
Or whose firm hands have held the plow
Or who will gather in the yield;
But I know it is my field now.

My eyes have watched the sun fall down
And gild the furrows with its light.
My feet have cut across from town
And worn a pathway on the right.

It does not matter in whose name
The deed is written. I divine
It is my field because the claim
On its enjoyment is all mine.

Summer Fields
Grace Noll Crowell

How green and bright they are! How still they lie!
The summer fields outstretching in the sun:
An emerald glory, sharp as any cry,
Dipping beneath the racing winds that run
Across the summer day on swift, light feet
To silver the little leaning, laughing grass,
To gild the tossing beads of ripening wheat.

Here is peace to store within the breast
Against the days of tumult and despair.
Within this cool, green light the heart can rest,
The body strengthens in the clear, clean air,
The soul grows tall, the viol-string tensions cease
Here in this summer stillness, summer peace.

Photographer Steve Terrill captured this view of the Palouse Grainfields from Steptoe Butte in Washington.

After the Storm

James W. Pool

The pattering of raindrops slowly fades
As parting thunder rumbles far away.
The lowering clouds retreat into the east,
And sky reveals the shining blue of day.

Now golden sunlight floods across the world,
Far brighter than before the bath of rain,
While birds resume their interrupted songs
And crickets raise a chirping, gay refrain.

As essence sweeter than a blooming bud
Comes softly drifting on the cooling breeze,
Smelling of rich, rejuvenated earth,
Of freshened fields, of grass and rain-washed trees.

On leaves and blades now turned to greet the sun
Shine jewels more beautiful than queens have worn
As all the purified and thirst-quenched earth
Rejoices in the gift of life reborn.

Triumphal arch, that fill'st the sky
When storms prepare to part,
I ask not proud Philosophy
To teach me what thou art.
                    — Thomas Campbell

*A rainbow arches over Oregon's Columbia River following
a summertime storm. Photo by Steve Terrill.*

Lansing Christman

Nature's Open Door

More than a century ago, American naturalist John Burroughs called summer "nature's door wide open." He wrote, "Go to the top of the hill on such a morning, see how unspeakably fresh the world looks." I have gone to the top of the hill on many such mornings, and I have found the same freshness in the sparkle of dew-covered grass, in the coolness of the dawn, and in the fragrance of the flowers. Everything seems so new, so fresh in the brightness of summer's dawn.

There is something in the summer evening too that gives me much the same outlook. I find comfort and solace in a summer twilight. I am moved by the transformation from daylight to darkness, the appearance of the stars, and the onset of night.

I am forever enchanted by the mysteries of darkness and its hidden secrets. Darkness seems to be whispering. I sit alone quietly on a bench in the yard, surrounded by grass and trees and shrubs, catching a note here and there of whatever sounds may come from field and wood. The heat of the day is gone. A soft, gentle breeze sweeps across my face. I muse and I listen. I hear the whippoorwill call from a distant wood. The cadence of tree frogs joins that of the crickets chirping in the yard. The low, resonating croaks of the bullfrogs beat a slow and rhythmic accompaniment from the pasture pond. The mockingbird sings repeating chords and then slips off into a deep silence.

I am comforted to know these magical sounds of nature will endure for the ages, all near at hand in woods and pastures, in orchards and bogs. For this brief hour, I am a part of whatever transpires around me: a firefly, a cricket, the stars, and the whisper of that cooling breeze sweeping through nature's wide-open door.

The author of three published books, Lansing Christman has been contributing to Ideals *for almost thirty years. Mr. Christman has also been published in several American, foreign, and braille anthologies. He lives in rural South Carolina.*

Twilight falls over a farm in Floyd County, Indiana. Photo by Daniel Dempster.

Father

Melvina Genoa Morris

Upon his shoulders weigh the stern demands
Of men and nations; but tall he stands,
   Firm and unfaltering.
A sovereign he, and to no royal hands
   Doth servile tribute bring.
Yet, see him bow, one threshold passing o'er
While all his pride's apparel falls before
Young eyes, who greet him, "Father," at the door
   Where love is king.

When a Man Turns Homeward

Daniel Whitehead Hicky

When a man turns homeward through the moonfall,
Swift in his path like a meteor bright,
Kindling his wonder and blinding his sight,
His feet will go on. His heartbeats will call
Deep in his breast like quick music, and all
The darkness that swirls like a flame of dead light
Cannot fetter his feet turned homeward at night.
Past thicket and trees like a towering wall
He will go on over hillside and stone,
Clinging like hope to the road that he knows.
Groping along like a shadow, alone,
He will reach for the latch where a candle, gold-eyed,
Watches with her for the door that will close,
Leaving the world like a kitten outside!

A hawthorn tree shades a fairy-tale cottage in Vashon Island, Washington.
Photo by Mary Liz Austin.

Left: Paula D'Agostino of East Haven, Connecticut, wanted us to enjoy this snapshot of her beach baby, granddaughter Jenna D'Agostino, age fourteen months. Jenna is ready for her next swim during a vacation to Grandpa's house in Florida.

Below left: The parents of little Emily McDaniel chose a patch of black-eyed Susans as the ideal backdrop for a photo of Emily in a favorite hat. The snapshot was sent to us by Emily's grandmother, Dee J. McDaniel of Scottsbluff, Nebraska.

Below right: Three-year-old Eddie Sives discovers the joys of a day at the lake with his granddad. This photo was sent to us by the little fisherman's mother, Elizabeth Sives of Quakertown, Pennsylvania.

Thank you Paula D'Agostino, Dee J. McDaniel, Elizabeth Sives, Linda M. Mutz, and Jane Frederick for sharing your family photographs with *Ideals*. We hope to hear from other readers who would like to share snapshots with the *Ideals* family. Please include a self-addressed, stamped envelope if you would like the photos returned. Keep your original photographs for safekeeping and send duplicate photos along with your name, address, and telephone number to:

Readers' Forum
Ideals Publications, Inc.
535 Metroplex Drive, Suite 250
Nashville, Tennessee 37211

Above: Linda M. Mutz of Binghamton, New York, often tells her granddaughter, Veronica, how special she is. When this picture was taken, three-year-old Veronica was admiring a flower bed, and Grandma Linda told her, "There are many black-eyed Susans, but only one of you."

Right: This sunny charmer is Emily Claire, age fifteen months, the granddaughter of Jane Frederick of Gadsden, Alabama. Emily's smile and sweet disposition make her dear to everyone she meets, especially her parents and her sister and brother.

Dear *Ideals*,

Perhaps you would like to print a picture of my dear little auburn-colored, loveable dog named Candy. She is a Dandie Dinmont breed—a charming, perky little Terrier. I take her on walks almost every day, and we have made many friends.

When I moved to my present area, I wondered who lived in the yellow home with the beautiful old-fashioned garden. It didn't take long to find out. Her name is Violet, and she lets Candy and me sit on her grass and enjoy the beauty of her many flowers. She very seldom lets me leave without giving me a bouquet. Violet is ninety-four years old now and is truly a darling person. When I wanted a special picture of Candy, whose home do you think came to mind? I think Candy thought it was the ideal home too. This picture is brimming with fond memories.

Joyce Jacobs
Logan, Utah

Dear *Ideals*,

While recently looking through my copies of *Ideals*, I found my hardback copy of *Sweetheart Ideals Volume 1*, published in Milwaukee, Wisconsin, and priced at two dollars. It is still in its original paper cover over the hardback. This *Sweetheart Ideals* was given to me on Valentine's Day in 1949 by my then boyfriend. We celebrated our fiftieth wedding anniversary last June.

Through the years, your copies of *Ideals* have always graced our bookshelves. I used pictures and poems from *Ideals* in my junior high English classes. Now my son and daughter, also teachers, use *Ideals* on their bulletin boards. Thank you for your inspirational publications over the years.

Mrs. Lou Casseday
Newbury, Ohio

ideals

Publisher, Patricia A. Pingry
Editor, Michelle Prater Burke
Designer, Travis Rader
Copy Editor, Elizabeth Kea
Contributing Editors, Lansing Christman, Deana Deck, Pamela Kennedy, and Nancy Skarmeas

ACKNOWLEDGMENTS
ALDIS, DOROTHY. "Feet" from *Sung under the Silver Umbrella"* (p.47). Reprinted by permission of the Association for Childhood Education International, 17904 Georgia Avenue, Suite 215, Olney, MD. Copyright 1946 by the Association. CROWELL, GRACE NOLL. "Summer Fields" from *Between Eternities* by Grace Noll Crowell, Copyright © 1944, renewed © 1972 by Reid Crowell. Reprinted by permission of HarperCollins Publishers, Inc. HOLMES, MARJORIE. Excerpt from "Elephants on Main Street" from *You and I and Yesterday* by Marjorie Holmes. Used by permission of the author. JAQUES, EDNA. "Old Farmer at the Five and Ten." Used by permission of the Estate of Edna Jaques. Used by permission of Branden Publishing. Our sincere thanks to the following author and publisher whom we were unable to locate: Jessie Lofgren Craft for "Summer Walk" from *Moods in Melody*, 1961, Dorrance & Company.

Dear Folks at *Ideals*,

I am sending a photo of my granddaughter Elizabeth Kopp. Elizabeth, who lives on a small farm less than a mile away from me, is four years old and enjoys taking greens, angleworms, and grasshoppers to the fence to feed the chickens. Whenever the chickens see her, they scurry to the fence. I thought you'd like to share this photo on the family page; I always enjoy seeing all the little ones in your beautiful magazine.

Mae E. Kopp
Beloit, Wisconsin